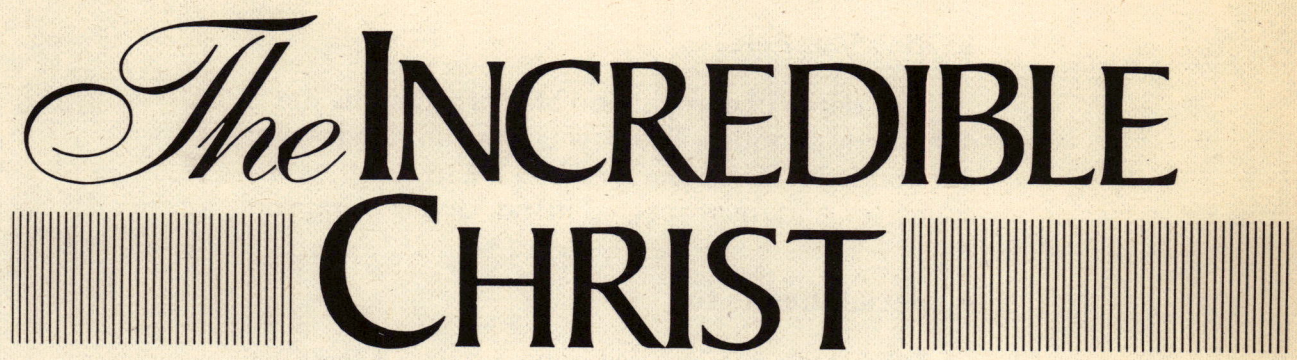

The INCREDIBLE CHRIST

Getting to Know Jesus—Life's Greatest Adventure

A practical workbook on living the Christian life to be used alone or in groups as a study guide.

ILLUSTRATED BY RICK BUNDSCHUH

Jim Burns

Harvest House Publishers
Eugene, Oregon 97402

Dedication:

To Rich Van Pelt...

Your depth of compassion always motivates me to rethink my priorities. Thank you for your friendship and the wonderful times together. You are my brother, my counselor, and my respected friend. God is using you!

A special thanks to:

Todd Dean, for your willingness to live a sacrificial life for the Kingdom, and for our growing partnership in ministry.

Jeanne Grantham, for doing a superb job of typing the manuscript. But more than that, for being the positive, upbeat, joyous Christian that you are.

The Incredible Christ

Copyright © 1987 by Harvest House Publishers
Eugene, Oregon 97402

ISBN 0-89081-575-5

All rights reserved. No portion of this book may be reproduced in any form without the written permission of the Publisher.

Printed in the United States of America.

Unless otherwise indicated, all Scripture quotations in this book are taken from the Holy Bible, New International Version, Copyright © 1978 by the New York International Bible Society. Used by permission.

Verses marked NASB are taken from the New American Standard Bible, © The Lockman Foundation 1960, 1962, 1963, 1968, 1971, 1972, 1973, 1975, 1977. Used by permission.

TABLE OF CONTENTS

Introduction

1. The Birth of Jesus Christ 5
2. The Incarnation of God. 10
3. The Baptism of Jesus 15
4. The Temptation in the Wilderness. 20
5. The Gathering of His Disciples 27
6. The Triumphal Entry 33
7. The Last Supper. .38
8. The Crucifixion of Jesus Christ. 43
9. The Death of Christ. 48
10. The Resurrection 53
11. The Great Commission. 60
12. The Ascension of Jesus 64

Introduction

When I started this project I had no idea of the great impact it would have on my life personally. Reading through and studying the life and events of Jesus Christ is one of the most challenging and wonderful experiences in my Christian life. In writing this book and looking at the major events of Jesus' life, I am constantly reminded of the unconditional and sacrificial love of God.

I love the old Russian proverb that says, "He who has this disease called Jesus Christ will never be cured." I am convinced that if you seriously study the life of Jesus you will never be the same. An encounter with Jesus Christ always makes our lives different. Sometimes it makes us uncomfortable—revealing to us a life-style grown stagnant—and other times it inspires us or gives us hope. My prayer for you is that as you examine these incredible occurrences in the life of Jesus you will catch a greater glimpse of the depth of His love and the strength of His commitment to you. My hope is that you will fall more in love with this God/man who suffered and died in order that we might be set free.

Therefore God exalted him to the highest place and gave him the name that is above every name, that at the name of Jesus every knee should bow, in heaven and on earth and under the earth, and every tongue confess that Jesus Christ is Lord, to the glory of God the Father.
Philippians 2:9-11

You will know the truth, and the truth will set you free.
John 8:32

Jim Burns
Dana Point, California

Other Books in the LifeSources for Youth Series

Christian Life Series
Putting God First
Making Your Life Count
Living Your Life...As God Intended
Giving Yourself to God
Christian Life Series Leader's Guide

Christian Growth Series
Commitment to Growth
Congratulations! You are Gifted!
Getting It Together
Building Relationships...with God and Others
Christian Growth Series Leader's Guide

Getting in Touch with God

Handling Your Hormones
Handling Your Hormones, the Straight Scoop on Love and Sexuality
Handling Your Hormones Involvement Guide
Handling Your Hormones Leader's Guide

Growth Unlimited: Discovering Intimacy with God

1. The Birth of Jesus Christ

I. THE EVENT

Read Luke 2:1-20.

After reading this great passage, what part of the story impresses you the most?

List the events in this passage that were supernatural, referring to those that could not happen unless God arranged them.

II. LOOKING AT THE EVENT

1. The Birth of Jesus Foretold

The Old Testament has a number of prophecies (foretellings of the future) about the birth of the Messiah, Jesus Christ. These prophecies were given to people by God hundreds of years before the birth of Jesus. Let us look at two of these prophecies.

Look up each Scripture and describe the Old Testament prophecy and New Testament fulfillment in the blank space given.

Old Testament Prophecy	New Testament Fulfillment
Micah 5:2	Matthew 2:1-6 John 7:42
Isaiah 7:14	Matthew 1:23

2. Mary and Joseph

Read Matthew 1:18-25.

If you were Joseph, how would you have reacted when Mary told you she was pregnant?

What factor influenced Joseph and made him change his mind?

3. Visit of the Wise Men

Read Matthew 2:1-12.

What circumstances led to the wise men visiting Jesus in Bethlehem? (See Matthew 2:1-8.)

What did they do when they arrived in Bethlehem? (See Matthew 1:9-12.)

What can you do today that is similar to what the wise men did when they saw Jesus almost 2,000 years ago?

III. THE BIRTH OF JESUS AND YOU

According to John 3:17, why was Jesus born on this earth?

How does the birth of Jesus almost 2,000 years ago affect your life today?

On the same day that Jesus was born, an angel appeared to a group of shepherds. Paraphrase what the angel said to them in Luke 2:10,11.

The angel brought news of great joy. How has the birth of Jesus given you joy? List several reasons for rejoicing that are meaningful to you personally.

The angel named the baby Jesus, meaning *the Lord saves*. What is so unique about a baby being the Saviour of the world?

2. The Incarnation of God

I. THE EVENT

In the beginning was the Word, and the Word was with God, and the Word was God. He was with God in the beginning. Through him all things were made; without him nothing was made that has been made. In him was life, and that life was the light of men. The light shines in the darkness, but the darkness has not understood it . . . . The Word became flesh and lived for a while among us. We have seen his glory, the glory of the one and only Son, who came from the Father, full of grace and truth.

John 1:1-5,14

The *Word* in the Scripture above represents Jesus. What can be learned about Jesus from this passage?

How does this Scripture relate to the story of the birth of Jesus?

Why is the event recorded in John 1:1-5,14 so important to the Christmas story?

II. LOOKING AT THE EVENT

This Word that creates and sustains the world has become a person!

1. The Creation

Read Genesis 1:1 and John 1:1.

What are the similarities between these two Scriptures?

What part did Jesus (the Word) have in the creation of the world, according to John 1:1-3?

2. Who is Jesus?

Many people get confused when they try to figure out exactly who Jesus really is. Is He God or is He man? He was born of the flesh. Mary gave birth to Him. There was a time and a place. Yet the Bible teaches He *was* from the beginning of time. To grasp this truth, you must remember that our finite minds cannot always comprehend the infinite God. However, the best way to understand is to learn what the word *incarnation* means and how it is described in Scripture.

Incarnation means "in the flesh." Jesus Christ is the Incarnation of God. He is the embodiment of God. Jesus is fully God and fully human. God visited earth in the form of a human person, Jesus.

So that the meaning of this may penetrate your heart, read the Scriptures below and write in your own words what they mean.

John 1:14

Colossians 1:15-20

Hebrews 2:17,18

After reflecting upon these Scriptures, summarize for yourself what the word *incarnation* means.

What makes this event, the Incarnation, such an important one to the world?

III. THE INCARNATION AND YOU

The Incarnation represents the ultimate act of God's love. God answered the question, "How do you package love?" by using a stable and straw.

The baby Jesus, born in a stable and straw, was fully human and fully God.

What makes this act of God a sign of deep love?

Why is it so difficult to comprehend God's unconditional love?

Read Hebrews 2:17,18 again.

How can Jesus identify with you?

How can this Scripture help you live your Christian life?

Each Christmas we are reminded that God's gift to us is Jesus in the flesh. Your gift to God should be your very life.

What areas of your life do you still need to give to God? Start today!

3. The Baptism of Jesus

I. THE EVENT

>   Then Jesus came from Galilee to the Jordan to be baptized by John. But John tried to deter him, saying, "I need to be baptized by you, and do you come to me?"
>   Jesus replied, "Let it be so now; it is proper for us to do this to fulfill all righteousness." Then John consented.
>   As soon as Jesus was baptized, he went up out of the water. At that moment heaven was opened, and he saw the Spirit of God descending like a dove and lighting on him. And a voice from heaven said, "This is my Son, whom I love; with him I am well pleased."
>
>   Matthew 3:13-17

Who baptized Jesus? What did the one who baptized Jesus say about the idea of doing so?

What was Jesus' response?

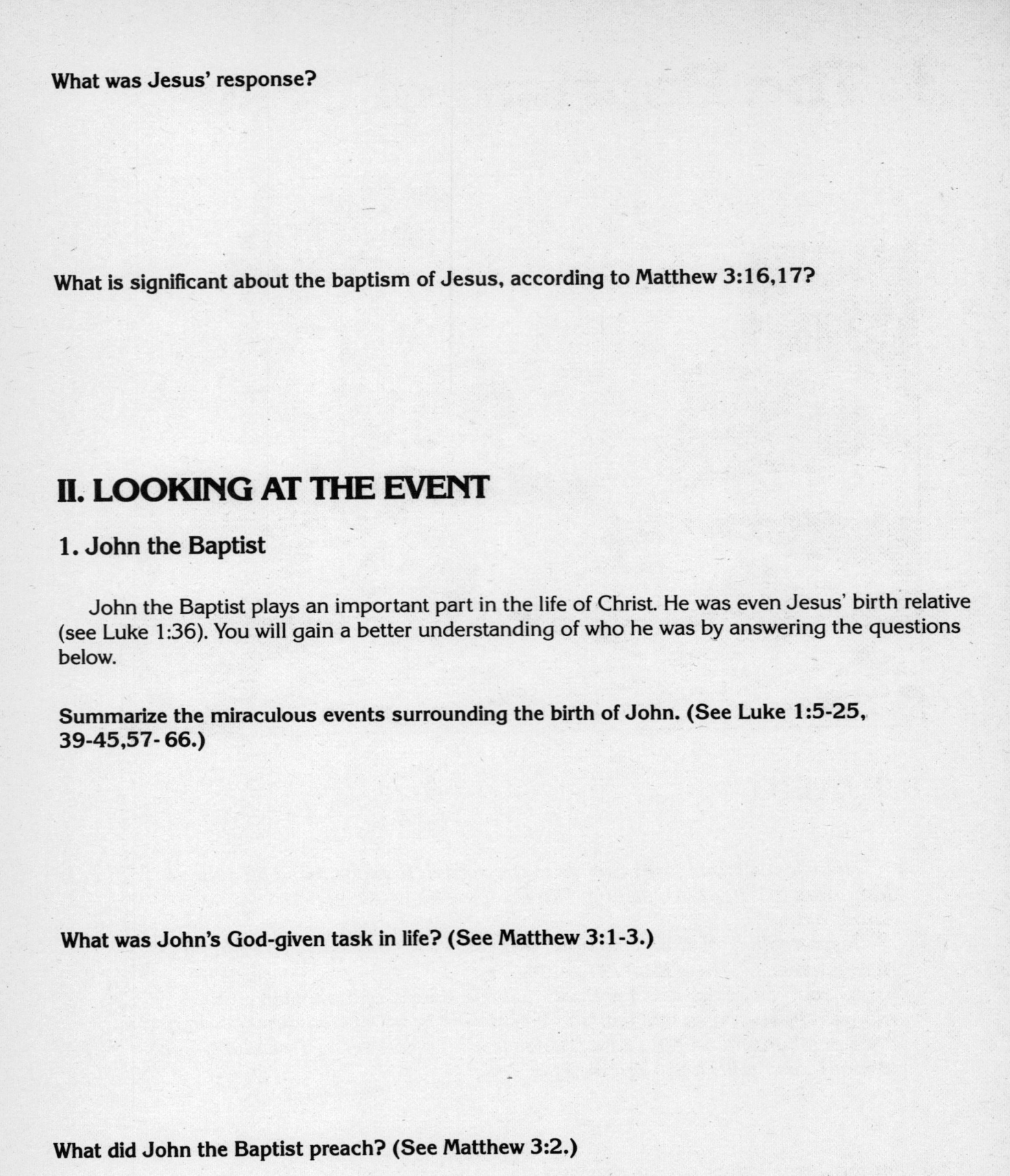

What is significant about the baptism of Jesus, according to Matthew 3:16,17?

II. LOOKING AT THE EVENT

1. John the Baptist

John the Baptist plays an important part in the life of Christ. He was even Jesus' birth relative (see Luke 1:36). You will gain a better understanding of who he was by answering the questions below.

Summarize the miraculous events surrounding the birth of John. (See Luke 1:5-25, 39-45, 57-66.)

What was John's God-given task in life? (See Matthew 3:1-3.)

What did John the Baptist preach? (See Matthew 3:2.)

Describe John's physical appearance. (See Matthew 3:4.)

What did John say to the people about Jesus and His baptism? (See Mark 1:7,8.)

2. The Baptism

Since baptism is a sign of repentance of sin, why do you suppose John was reluctant to baptize Jesus? (See Matthew 3:13,14.)

What did John the Baptist say as he saw Jesus coming to be baptized? (See John 1:29-31.)

What is so significant about these words that John the Baptist spoke?

Read Matthew 3:16,17. What miraculous experiences took place at the baptism of Jesus?

What makes this event so significant in the life and ministry of Jesus Christ?

III. THE BAPTISM OF JESUS AND YOU

What does your baptism mean to you?[1]

---

1. If you have never been baptized, perhaps you should talk with your minister about this important matter.

Baptism signifies a new life and a new beginning. How does 2 Corinthians 5:1 relate to the new life available in Christ?

Baptism also signifies *repentance.* Repentance means to turn away from your sin and dedicate yourself to go in God's direction. Repentance is a continual act of turning our lives over to God.

List three areas of your life you would like to turn over to God.

   1.

   2.

   3.

God chose Jesus' baptism to be the symbol of a tremendous change in Jesus' life; the beginning of His public ministry. Take some time today to reflect on your baptism and the significance it has in your life and ministry.

4. The Temptation in the Wilderness

I. THE EVENT

Then Jesus was led by the Spirit into the desert to be tempted by the devil. After fasting forty days and forty nights, he was hungry. The tempter came to him and said, "If you are the Son of God, tell these stones to become bread."

Jesus answered, "It is written: 'Man does not live on bread alone, but on every word that comes from the mouth of God.'"

Then the devil took him to the holy city and had him stand on the highest point of the temple. "If you are the Son of God," he said, "throw yourself down. For it is written:

"'He will command his angels concerning you, and they will lift you up in their hands, so that you will not strike your foot against a stone.'"

Jesus answered him, "It is also written: 'Do not put the Lord your God to the test.'"

Again, the devil took him to a very high mountain and showed him all the kingdoms of the world and their splendor. "All this I will give you," he said, "if you will bow down and worship me."

Jesus said to him, "Away from me, Satan! For it is written: 'Worship the Lord your God, and serve him only.'"

Then the devil left him, and angels came and attended him.

Matthew 4:1-11

This extraordinary and essential story is part of Jesus' own autobiography. We must approach this story with a unique reverence, because in it Jesus is laying bare His most inner heart and soul. In the wilderness Jesus was alone. No one was with Him while He struggled with Satan's attempts to lure Him into temptation.

Why do you suppose Christ went immediately from His baptism to His 40-day experience in the wilderness?

21

In each exchange that Jesus had with Satan, He quoted from the book of Deuteronomy. We can get a better understanding of each temptation as we discover why Jesus quoted these particular passages. On the chart below write out what the three different temptations were and how Jesus chose to combat each temptation. Then write out what you think the passage means.

	Temptation	Jesus' Response	Meaning
1.			
2.			
3.			

II. LOOKING AT THE EVENT

What is Satan called in Matthew 4:3?

The biblical meaning of the word *tempt* is actually more closely related to the idea of being "tested." The wilderness temptation was a true test of Jesus' faith. As we investigate this story, we can find many insights for our own lives as we deal with temptations and testings of our faith.

Let us investigate the three responses listed in the chart above.

Man does not live on bread alone, but on every word that comes from the mouth of God.

What does this statement mean?

How is the response important in helping you overcome temptation?

Do not put the Lord your God to the test.

What does this statement mean?

How is this response important in helping you overcome temptation?

Have you ever put the Lord to a test? If so, what did you learn from the experience?

Away from me, Satan! For it is written: 'Worship the Lord your God and serve him only.'

What does this statement mean?

How is this response important in helping you overcome temptation?

How does James 4:7,8 relate to Jesus' statement?

III. THE TEMPTATION IN THE WILDERNESS AND YOU

If you could summarize the temptations in your life with one word, it would probably be *compromise*. It seems that in our world today we are continually challenged to compromise our beliefs and values.

Satan tempted Jesus to compromise His life for selfish power. Jesus showed us we can never defeat evil by compromising, by meeting evil halfway. In this wilderness experience, He laid down an excellent example for us. "Christianity cannot stoop to the level of the world; it must lift the world to its own level. Nothing else will do."[1]

Everyone struggles with compromise. What areas of your life are most difficult for you when it comes to compromising what you know to be the right thing to do?

---

1. William Barclay, *The Daily Study Bible*, vol. 1, *The Gospel of Matthew* (Philadelphia, PA: Westminster Press, 1975), p. 70.

What is the best way to combat your temptations?

Relate what you think Paul meant when he wrote:

No temptation has seized you except what is common to man. And God is faithful; he will not let you be tempted beyond what you can bear. But when you are tempted, he will also provide a way out so that you can stand up under it.

1 Corinthians 10:13

Jesus used Scripture to respond to Satan's temptations. How can the use of Scripture aid you in overcoming temptation?

Here is a list of Scriptures to help you win the fight with temptation. For greatest benefit, memorize these reassuring promises from God.

Circle the ones that relate most to you.

Delight yourself in the Lord, and he will give you the desires of your heart.

Psalm 37:4

And we know that in all things God works for the good of those who love Him, who have been called according to his purpose.

Romans 8:28

But you will receive power when the Holy Spirit comes on you; and you will be my witnesses in Jerusalem, and in Judea and Samaria, and to the ends of the earth.

Acts 1:8

If any of you lacks wisdom, he should ask God, who gives generously to all without finding fault, and it will be given to him.

James 1:5

Being confident of this, that he who began a good work in you will carry it on to completion until the day of Christ Jesus.

Philippians 1:6

And my God will meet all your needs according to his glorious riches in Christ Jesus.

Philippians 4:19

5. The Gathering of His Disciples

I. THE EVENT

As Jesus was walking beside the Sea of Galilee, he saw two brothers, Simon called Peter and his brother Andrew. They were casting a net into the lake, for they were fishermen. "Come, follow me," Jesus said, "and I will make you fishers of men." At once they left their nets and followed him.

Going on from there, he saw two other brothers, James son of Zebedee and his brother John. They were in a boat with their father Zebedee, preparing their nets. Jesus called them, and immediately they left the boat and their father and followed him.

Matthew 4:18-22

What did Jesus say to Peter and Andrew when He invited them to be His disciples? (See v. 19.)

What did James and John do in response to the call of Jesus? (See v. 22.)

II. LOOKING AT THE EVENT

It is important to note that Jesus' phrase "follow me" was a common one; it implied that He was calling them to be *permanent* disciples. If the disciples followed Jesus they were giving up their professions, their homes, and at times even their finances. This call definitely did not come on the first chance meeting with Jesus. He had developed a relationship with His disciples before He called them to follow Him.

What is the significance of Jesus' call recorded in Matthew 4:19?

What did the disciples sacrifice in order to follow Jesus?

The disciples of Jesus were from all walks of life. Matthew, sometimes called Levi, was a tax collector called to follow Jesus. He was known as a traitor because he was a Jew who collected taxes from his fellow Jews for the Roman government. Tax collectors were looked upon as despised sinners.

Read Luke 5:27-32.

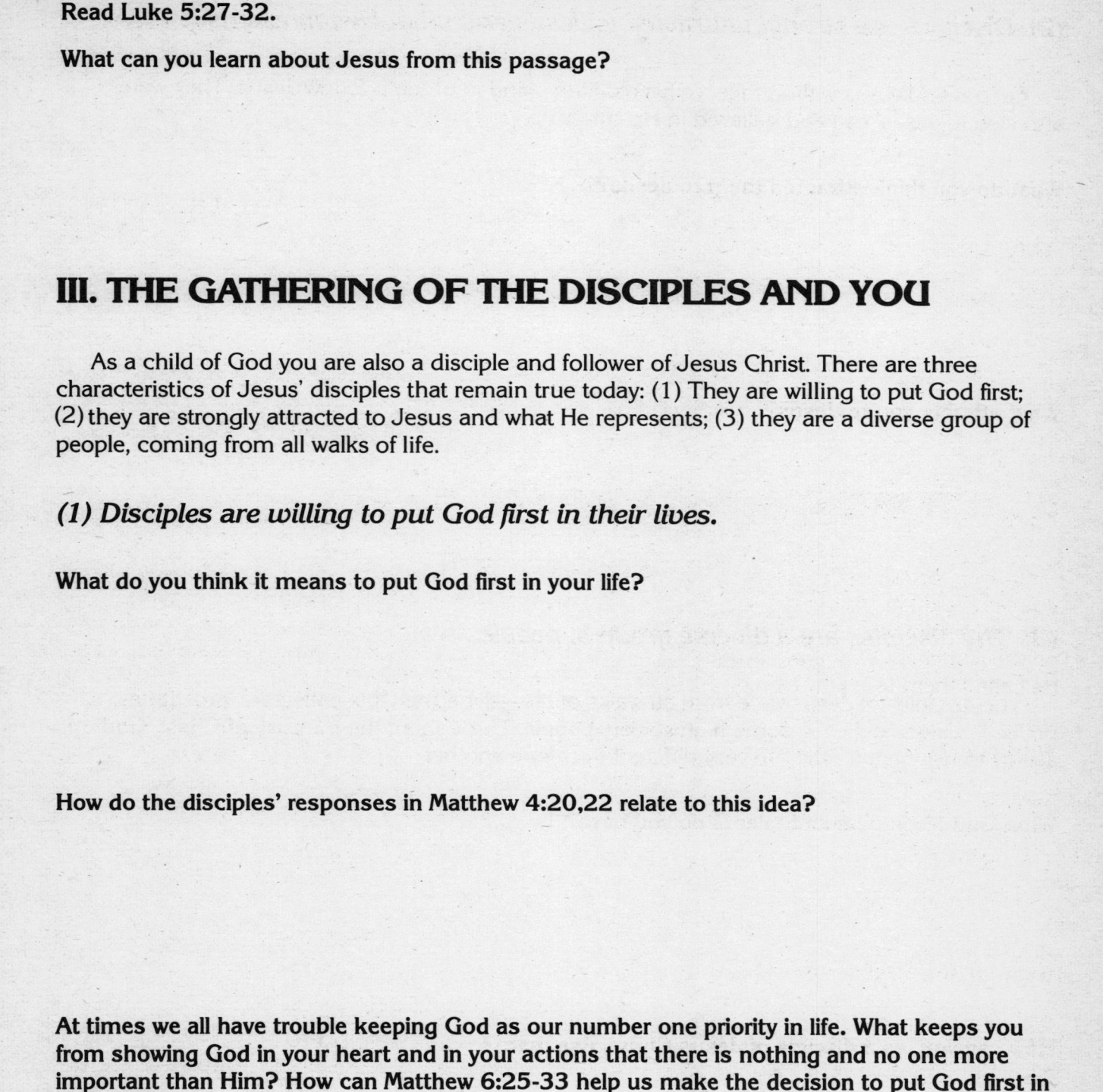

What can you learn about Jesus from this passage?

III. THE GATHERING OF THE DISCIPLES AND YOU

As a child of God you are also a disciple and follower of Jesus Christ. There are three characteristics of Jesus' disciples that remain true today: (1) They are willing to put God first; (2) they are strongly attracted to Jesus and what He represents; (3) they are a diverse group of people, coming from all walks of life.

(1) Disciples are willing to put God first in their lives.

What do you think it means to put God first in your life?

How do the disciples' responses in Matthew 4:20,22 relate to this idea?

At times we all have trouble keeping God as our number one priority in life. What keeps you from showing God in your heart and in your actions that there is nothing and no one more important than Him? How can Matthew 6:25-33 help us make the decision to put God first in our lives?

(2) Disciples are strongly attracted to Jesus and what He represents.

Each disciple was willing to leave his old life behind in order to follow Jesus. They were attracted to Jesus' call and believed in His ministry.

What do you think attracted them to Jesus?

What attracts you to Jesus?

(3) The disciples are a diverse group of people.

The disciples of Jesus were from all walks of life—fishermen, tax collectors, prostitutes, political zealots and even some high society people. Throughout the ministry of Christ, God seems to use people who are very different from one another.

What God-given gifts and talents do you have?

How can you, as a disciple of Jesus Christ, use them?

Read Romans 12:4-8.

How does this relate to the idea of diversity in the Body of Christ?

The Influence of Jesus Christ

The influence of Jesus has continued, reaching far beyond His first disciples. He is still gathering disciples today and touching our world. Here is a beautiful piece written about the powerful effect of Christ's life.

> Here is a man who was born in an obscure village, the child of a peasant woman. He grew up in another village. He worked in a carpenter shop until He was thirty, and then for three years He was an itinerant preacher. He never wrote a book. He never held an office. He never owned a home. He never had a family. He never went to college. He never put His feet inside a big city. He never traveled two hundred miles from the place where He was born. He never did one of the things that usually accompany greatness. He had no credentials but Himself.
>
> While still a young man, the tide of popular opinion turned against Him. His friends ran away. One of them denied Him. He was turned over to His enemies. He went through the mockery of a trial. He was nailed upon a cross between two thieves. His executioners gambled for the only piece of property He had on earth while He was dying. When He was dead He was taken down and laid in a borrowed grave through the pity of a friend.
>
> Nineteen wide centuries have come and gone, and today He is the centerpiece of the human race and the leader of the column of progress.
>
> I am far within the mark when I say that all the armies that ever marched, and all the navies that were ever built, and all the parliaments that ever sat, and all the kings that ever reigned, put together have not affected the life of man upon this earth as has that one solitary life.[1]

How do you feel when you read about the effect of Christ's life on our world?

---

1. Source unknown, public domain.

How can Christ use your life to influence others in a positive and life-changing direction?

Today Jesus is calling, *Come, follow me, and I will make you fishers of men* (Matthew 4:19). What does that mean to you personally, and what are you willing to do about the call?

6. The Triumphal Entry

I. THE EVENT

After Jesus had said this, he went on ahead, going up to Jerusalem. As he approached Bethphage and Bethany at the hill called the Mount of Olives, he sent two of his disciples, saying to them, "Go to the village ahead of you, and as you enter it, you will find a colt tied there, which no one has ever ridden. Untie it and bring it here. If anyone asks you, 'Why are you untying it?' tell him, 'The Lord needs it.'"

Those who were sent ahead went and found it just as he had told them. As they were untying the colt, its owners asked them, "Why are you untying the colt?"

They replied, "The Lord needs it."

They brought it to Jesus, threw their cloaks on the colt and put Jesus on it. As he went along, people spread their cloaks on the road.

When he came near the place where the road goes down the Mount of

Olives, the whole crowd of disciples began joyfully to praise God in loud voices for all the miracles they had seen:

"Blessed is the king who comes in the name of the Lord!"

"Peace in heaven and glory in the highest!"

Some of the Pharisees in the crowd said to Jesus, "Teacher, rebuke your disciples!"

"I tell you," he replied, "if they keep quiet, the stones will cry out."

Luke 19:28-40

Jesus made His public entry in Jerusalem on a day that we know as Palm Sunday. It was a day of victory and rejoicing. People in the crowd praised Jesus as He entered Jerusalem. Probably no one realized that in less than a week many of them would also watch Him die on the cross, executed alongside common criminals.

List the events that took place on the occasion of the triumphal entry of Jesus into Jerusalem.

II. LOOKING AT THE EVENTS

Before Jesus was to go into Jerusalem to celebrate the Passover, He asked His disciples to go to a nearby village (probably Bethphage) and get a donkey's colt for Him to ride into the city. He assumed that permission would be given to use the colt. How he knew the owner of the colt no one really knows.

**What is the great significance of Jesus riding on the colt into Jerusalem?
(See Matthew 21:1-7.)**

What did the crowds do as Jesus came riding into Jerusalem, according to Scripture found in Matthew 21:8 and Mark 11:8?

34

For the Hebrew people the palm was the symbol of beauty and righteousness. It signified the "king" and was always associated with rejoicing as well as triumph and victory.

What does Psalm 92:12-14 tell us about the palm?

How does the above Scripture in the Psalms, and the fact that the people placed the branches on the road before Jesus, help us understand how many of the people felt about Jesus?

What did the crowds shout, according to Matthew 21:9 and Mark 11:9,10?

"*Hosanna* means *Save now!* and it was the cry for help which a people in distress addressed to their king or their god."[1]

How is Psalm 118:25 similar to the plea of the people honoring Jesus?

Why do you think the crowd responded in such a positive manner to Jesus?

---

2. William Barclay, *The Daily Study Bible*, vol. 2, *The Gospel of Matthew* (Philadelphia, PA: Westminster Press, 1977), p. 239.

III. THE TRIUMPHAL ENTRY AND YOU

Imagine yourself in the crowd honoring Jesus as He entered Jerusalem. What thoughts would have been on your mind as you cried out, *Hosanna* [Save Now] . . . . *Blessed is he who comes in the name of the Lord!"* (Matthew 21:9)?

Now imagine yourself a few days later and this time many of the same people who praised and blessed Jesus were shouting, *Crucify him! . . . Crucify him!* (Mark 15:13,14). What kinds of emotions would you feel?

A few days after the Crucifixion you now begin to hear rumors that Jesus has been raised from the dead. His disciples have seen Him, and more than 500 people also claim to have seen Him. What would you be thinking and feeling?

The triumphal entry of Jesus was a key event in His life. It is unique because He allowed Himself to be worshipped and called the King.

Take some time and reread this beautiful event, then write down your own praise to God. Completing the sentences below will help you in this.

I worship God because

I honor God because

I praise God because

I thank God because

He is worthy to be called King and Lord because

7. The Last Supper

I. THE EVENT

On the first day of the Feast of Unleavened Bread, the disciples came to Jesus and asked, "Where do you want us to make preparations for you to eat the Passover?"

He replied, "Go into the city to a certain man and tell him, 'The Teacher says: My appointed time is near. I am going to celebrate the Passover with my disciples at your house.'" So the disciples did as Jesus had directed them and prepared the Passover.

When evening came, Jesus was reclining at the table with the Twelve. And while they were eating, he said, "I tell you the truth, one of you will betray me."

They were very sad and began to say to him one after the other, "Surely not I, Lord?"

Jesus replied, "The one who has dipped his hand into the bowl with me *will betray me. The Son of Man will go just as it is written about him. But woe to that man who betrays the Son of Man! It would be better for him if he had not been born."*

Then Judas, the one who would betray him, said, "Surely not I, Rabbi?"

Jesus answered, "Yes, it is you."

While they were eating, Jesus took bread, gave thanks and offered it to them, saying, "Drink from it, all of you. This is my blood of the covenant, which is poured out for many for the forgiveness of sins. I tell you, I will not drink of this fruit of the vine from now on until that day when I drink it anew with you in my Father's kingdom."

Matthew 26:17-29

Why is this event commonly called the "Last Supper?"

Why do you suppose this meal that Jesus had with His disciples would be considered a major event in His life?

II. LOOKING AT THE EVENT

1. The Passover Meal

Jesus was coming into the holy city of Jerusalem in order to participate in the sacred Passover celebration. To gain a better understanding of what Christians call Communion or the *Eucharist,* we must understand a little of the Passover meal eaten at the Last Supper of Jesus before His crucifixion.

Read Exodus 12 in order to grasp what the Passover celebration is all about. Summarize the Passover in your own words in the space below.

2. Judas's Betrayal Foretold

What did Jesus say about the person who would betray Him? (See Matthew 26:20-25.)

What took place in Matthew 26:47-50 and Matthew 27:3-5?

3. The Lord's Supper Instituted

How were Jesus Christ's words, recorded in Matthew 26:26-29, a prophecy of His death?

What is the significance of Scripture regarding bread? Regarding wine?

Why is Communion (the Eucharist) as special today as it was almost 2,000 years ago?

III. THE LAST SUPPER AND YOU

Many of the events of Jesus' life were recorded in the New Testament, but the Last Supper is the only one recreated and remembered daily by Christians all over the earth. Participating in Communion is an act of remembrance that Jesus Christ's body was broken for you. He died so that you might live. It also means remembering that His blood was shed for you so that your sins would be forgiven. You are righteous before God only because of the broken Body and Blood of Jesus Christ.

When you realize that many thousands of Christians all over the world share with you in Communion, how do you feel?

What makes Communion special for you? If it is not special to you, if it has simply been a ritual, write down your feelings about that.

Communion can be a profound time—an intimate encounter with God. When we participate in the Eucharist meal, Christ is present. Once again we are reminded of His sacrificial love for us.

The next time you approach the Communion table, here are some things to think about:

1. Communion is a time of *reflection*—reflecting on all that God has done for you and on His awesome demonstration of love. Take a few moments to reflect, then write down your thoughts in the space below.

2. Communion is a time of *confession.* **When we stand in the presence of Christ we must confess our sins and shortcomings. To confess our sins to God means to agree with Him that we miss the mark of His perfection, and need Him to be our Saviour and Forgiver. Take some time to confess your sins to God. You may write them in the space below if you wish.**

When you are finished confessing your sins, read 1 John 1:9. What is the good news of this verse?

3. Communion is a time of *dedication.* **Whenever we are aware of the ultimate sacrifice of love, Christ shedding His blood and dying on a cross on our behalf, we are drawn to dedicate our life to Him and to be reconciled to Him. Take a few moments to pray. Tell God of your love for Him and your commitment to Him.**

4. Communion is a time of *praise.* **We can praise and thank God for His unconditional love. Communion reminds us of His kindness and goodness to our sinful world. Write in the space below your praise to God.**

Let everything that has breath praise the Lord.

Psalm 150:6

8. The Crucifixion of Jesus Christ

I. THE EVENT

    Then the governor's soldiers took Jesus into the Praetorium and gathered the whole company of soldiers around him. They stripped him and put a scarlet robe on him, and then wove a crown of thorns and set it on his head. They put a staff in his right hand and knelt in front of him and mocked him. "Hail, King of the Jews!" they said. They spit on him, and took the staff and struck him on the head again and again. After they had mocked him, they took off the robe and put his own clothes on him. Then they led him away to crucify him.
    As they were going out, they met a man from Cyrene, named Simon, and

they forced him to carry the cross. They came to a place called Golgotha (which means The Place of the Skull). There they offered him wine to drink, mixed with gall; but after tasting it, he refused to drink it. When they had crucified him, they divided up his clothes by casting lots. And sitting down, they kept watch over him there. Above his head they placed the written charge against him: THIS IS JESUS, THE KING OF THE JEWS. Two robbers were crucified with him, one on his right and one on his left. Those who passed by hurled insults at him, shaking their heads and saying, "You who are going to destroy the temple and build it in three days, save yourself! Come down from the cross, if you are the Son of God!"

In the same way the chief priests, the teachers of the law and the elders mocked him. "He saved others," they said, "but he can't save himself! He's the king of Israel! Let him come down now from the cross, and we will believe in him. He trusts in God. Let God rescue him now if he wants him, for he said, 'I am the Son of God.'" In the same way the robbers who were crucified with him also heaped insults on him.

Matthew 27:27-44*

Crucifixion (hanging on a cross) was the Roman method of execution for slaves and foreigners. Generally it took a very long time for a person to die on a cross, therefore making it excruciatingly painful. Death by crucifixion was unspeakably shameful and degrading. Yet Jesus Christ willingly suffered through the physical pain of the cross and the humility of the cross in order for humankind to be set free from sin.

After reading about the crucifixion of Jesus Christ, write out some of your feelings and impressions.

Jesus was physically beaten and mocked before He was crucified (see Matthew 27:27-31). If you were Jesus how would you have felt?

*Also see Mark 15:16-32; Luke 23:26-43; John 19:16-27

II. LOOKING AT THE EVENT

From reading the different accounts of the Crucifixion, what new insights do you gain from the other Gospels?

Mark 15:16-32

Luke 23:26-43

John 19:16-27

1. The Thief and Jesus

Read Luke 23:39-43.

What do you think Jesus meant when He said *Today you will be with me in paradise* (v. 43)?

What implications does this conversation have for our lives today?

2. The Event Foretold

Compare Matthew 27:35 and Psalm 22:16-18.

Psalm 22 was written hundreds of years before the crucifixion of Jesus, yet it contains amazingly detailed prophecy of what happened at the cross.

Read Psalm 22 and jot down any similarities you see to the crucifixion of Jesus.

How does looking at these similarities affect your faith in God?

III. THE CRUCIFIXION AND YOU

If you were one of the disciples of Jesus and you watched Him first being mocked and physically beaten, then struggling to carry the cross to Golgotha, and finally, hanging on that cross suffering, what thoughts would be going on in your mind?

How does the knowledge of Christ suffering on the cross help you to understand the depth of love He has for you?

Read 1 Peter 2:21-25. How does this Scripture help you better understand Christ's suffering for you?

What do you think verse 21 means?

Reread verse 24. How does this verse summarize the entire chapter on the crucifixion of Jesus?

9. The Death of Christ

I. THE EVENT

At the sixth hour darkness came over the whole land until the ninth hour. And at the ninth hour Jesus cried out in a loud voice, "Eloi, Eloi, lama sabachthani?"—which means, "My God, my God, why have you forsaken me?"

When some of those standing near heard this, they said, "Listen, he's calling Elijah."

One man ran, filled a sponge with wine vinegar, put it on a stick, and offered it to Jesus to drink. "Leave him alone now. Let's see if Elijah comes to take him down," he said.

With a loud cry, Jesus breathed his last.

The curtain of the temple was torn in two from top to bottom. And when the centurion, who stood there in front of Jesus, heard his cry and saw how he died, he said, "Surely this man was the Son of God!"

Some women were watching from a distance. Among them were Mary Magdalene, Mary the mother of James the younger and of Joses, and Salome. In Galilee these women had followed him and cared for his needs. Many other women who had come up with him to Jerusalem were also there.

It was Preparation Day (that is, the day before the Sabbath). So as evening approached, Joseph of Arimathea, a prominent member of the Council, who was himself waiting for the kingdom of God, went boldly to Pilate and asked for Jesus' body. Pilate was surprised to hear that he was already dead. Summoning the centurion, he asked him if Jesus had already died. When he learned from the centurion that it was so, he gave the body to Joseph. So Joseph bought some linen cloth, took down the body, wrapped it in the linen, and placed it in a tomb cut out of rock. Then he rolled a stone against the entrance of the tomb. Mary Magdalene and Mary the mother of Joses saw where he was laid.

Mark 15:33-47

It is incredible how God took one of the darkest moments in world history and turned it into the greatest demonstration of love and hope the world has ever known.

According to Mark 15:34 (see also Psalm 22:11), Jesus cried out with a loud voice, *My God, My God, why have you forsaken me?* **Why do you think He said that, and what did He mean by these words?**

Why do you suppose the Roman centurion made the statement recorded in Mark 15:39?

Using your imagination, write out a few thoughts on what the people in verse 40 might have been doing or talking about at this time.

II. LOOKING AT THE EVENT

1. Why Christ Died

Let us look at the following verses to discover and explore the purpose of Christ's death on the cross. After each section of Scripture, fill in the blanks below with your understanding of why Christ died.

Romans 5:6-8

Romans 3:21-25

John 3:16

2. The Result of the Death of Christ

Because Jesus Christ sacrificed His life on the cross almost 2,000 years ago, you have the opportunity to be set free from your sins and be called a child of God. Jesus Christ had to bear the sins of the world while on the cross to bridge the gap between the holiness of God and the sinfulness of humankind.

Here are a few "theological" words that will help you comprehend the meaning of the death of Jesus Christ.

Justification—"to be made right."
Justification refers to the believer's relationship with God. Because of Christ's death, the believer in Christ can be made right with God. An easy to way to remember what it means is to think of it as "just-as-if-I'd-never-sinned." You as a believer are justified and righteous before God, not because of your good works but because of Christ's sacrifice on the cross.

Read Romans 5:1. What is the result of being justified in Christ?

Atonement—"to cover or pardon."

Atonement is another way of saying your sins are forgiven. Christ paid the price of death in order for you to be spiritually alive. Your atonement as a believer means that your guilt and sin have been removed. Christ's death on the cross (the shedding of blood) took the place of your spiritual death, and set you free.

In the Old Testament the "Day of Atonement" was one of the major religious days of the year. Read Leviticus 16:29-34. What happened on this day, according to verse 30?

How often were the people's sins atoned for, or forgiven, according to verse 34?

How has the death of Christ in the New Testament become our Atonement? Read 2 Corinthians 5:21 and 1 Peter 2:24.

The New Testament form of atonement is *reconciliation*. Reconciliation means to change a person from enmity to friendship. According to Colossians 1:19-22, how has the process of reconciliation taken place for you?

THE DEATH OF CHRIST AND YOU

According to 1 Peter 3:18, why did Christ die?

How does Ephesians 2:8,9 fit in to this understanding of the death of Christ?

What can you do in order for the death of Christ to become relevant to your life?

Over nineteen hundred years ago in an obscure land, one man died a common criminal's death on a cross. Yet that one man's death has affected more lives than all of the other deaths before and after His. How has His death made an impact on your life?

10. The Resurrection

I. THE EVENT

After the Sabbath, at dawn on the first day of the week, Mary Magdalene and the other Mary went to look at the tomb.
There was a violent earthquake, for an angel of the Lord came down from heaven and, going to the tomb, rolled back the stone and sat on it. His appearance was like lightning, and his clothes were white as snow. The guards were so afraid of him that they shook and became like dead men.
The angel said to the women, "Do not be afraid, for I know that you are looking for Jesus, who was crucified. He is not here; he has risen, just as he said. Come and see the place where he lay."

Matthew 28:1-6

Early on the first day of the week, while it was still dark, Mary of Magdala went to the tomb and saw that the stone had been removed from the entrance. So she came running to Simon Peter and the other disciple, the one

Jesus loved, and said, "They have taken the Lord out of the tomb, and we don't know where they have put him."

So Peter and the other disciple started for the tomb. Both were running, but the other disciple outran Peter and reached the tomb first. He bent over and looked in at the strips of linen lying there but did not go in. Then Simon Peter, who was behind him, arrived and went into the tomb. He saw the strips of linen lying there, as well as the burial cloth that had been around Jesus' head. The cloth was folded up by itself, separate from the linen. Finally the other disciple, who had reached the tomb first, also went inside. He saw and believed.

John 20:1-8*

Summarize these two passages in one sentence.

*Also see Matthew 28:7-15; Mark 16:1-11; Luke 24:1-12; John 20:9-18

Imagine you are Mary Magdalene entering the empty tomb, and an angel of God says to you, *Do not be afraid, for I know that you are looking for Jesus, who was crucified. He is not here; he has risen, just as he said. Come and see the place where he lay* (Matthew 28:5,6). How would you feel? What thoughts would go through your mind?

II. LOOKING AT THE EVENT

1. The Significance of the Resurrection of Jesus Christ

The most important event in human history is the resurrection of Jesus Christ. This single miracle has transformed the history of the world like no other.

The Christian faith rests on the *fact* that Jesus Christ actually rose from the dead. Based upon this knowledge, we can be assured of the following:

- All He claimed about Himself must be true;

- All He said about life must be true;

- Our sins are forgiven. There is new life in the resurrection of Christ;

- Christians have eternal life, and will be resurrected from the dead just as Christ was.

What does Paul say about the Resurrection, according to 1 Corinthians 15:17-19?

If Jesus actually rose from the dead on the third day, what significance does that have to your faith?

What hope does the Resurrection give you?

Read John 11:25,26. How does Jesus' statement deal with the impact of the Resurrection on your life?

2. The Facts of the Resurrection

In order to believe in the resurrection of Jesus, you need not commit intellectual suicide. There are actually a number of facts that are unexplainable if Jesus did *not* actually rise from the dead. Let us explore these facts.

Fact One: Jesus foretold His Resurrection.

Read Matthew 16:21 and Matthew 17:22,23.

Why were the disciples distressed at the words of Jesus?

If Jesus did not rise from the dead on the third day, these verses from Matthew would make Him out to be a liar!

Fact Two: The testimony of eye witnesses and the transformation of the disciples can be explained logically only by the Resurrection appearance of Jesus.

At the Crucifixion the followers of Jesus were in despair. Their hopes for a Messiah were crushed. Yet after three days their lives were *transformed.*

Read 1 Corinthians 15:3-8. List those to whom Paul claims Jesus appeared after He was raised from the dead.[1]

There is no doubt that the disciples' lives were changed after the Resurrection appearance. According to Matthew 26:69-75, what did Peter do immediately before the Resurrection?

After the resurrection of Jesus what did Peter proclaim, as recorded in Acts 2:14-37?

Fact Three: The Resurrection is the only explanation for the empty tomb.

Many people throughout history have tried to disprove the Resurrection. It is true that if the resurrection of Jesus can be disproved, then the cornerstone of the Christian faith would be destroyed.

What were the precautions taken, both by the friends of Jesus and by His enemies, to ensure that His body would not be stolen?

His friends—Mark 15:46:

His enemies—Matthew 27:62-66:

---

1. For further study and a more comprehensive look at the Resurrection appearance, you may want to investigate other Scriptures: Matthew 28:1-20; Luke 24:13-53; John 20:19-29; John 21:1-14.

Listed below are the most common theories that skeptics throughout history have used to refute the Resurrection. Using the Scriptures you have looked at in this chapter so far, show the fallacy of these theories.

(1) The disciples stole and hid the body.

(2) The Roman or Jewish authorities took the body.

(3) Jesus never died. He walked out of the tomb.

(4) The women and disciples went to the wrong tomb.

(5) The disciples simply hallucinated that Jesus rose from the dead.

Fact Four: The Resurrection is the reason for the beginning of the Christian Church and for its rapid growth.

Within a very short time period the Christian faith spread all over the Roman Empire and beyond. The disciples of Jesus always spoke of the resurrected and living Christ.

What was the main subject of Peter's sermon found in Acts 2:29-32?

What was the response of Peter's audience, according to Acts 2:37-42?

III. THE RESURRECTION AND YOU

As Christians you have the power of the Resurrection living in you. Because of the resurrection of Jesus you can have hope for today and for eternity.

How can the resurrection of Jesus affect your life today?

What will you do differently because you know the power of His Resurrection?

Take a few moments to summarize what you have learned from this chapter about the resurrection of Jesus Christ.

11. The Great Commission

I. THE EVENT

Then the eleven disciples went to Galilee, to the mountain where Jesus had told them to go. When they saw him, they worshiped him; but some doubted. Then Jesus came to them and said, "All authority in heaven and on earth has been given to me. Therefore go and make disciples of all nations, baptizing them in the name of the Father and of the Son and of the Holy Spirit, and teaching them to obey everything I have commanded you. And surely I will be with you always, to the very end of the age.

Matthew 28:16-20

II. LOOKING AT THE EVENT

After the resurrection of Jesus, His disciples returned to Galilee where Jesus said He would meet them. While in Galilee He gave His disciples the Great Commission just before ascending into heaven.

Each part of the Great Commission had real significance to the disciples, and has just as much relevance to you, His disciple, today.

Let us investigate each section of the Great Commission and write out why it is significant.[1]

All authority in heaven and on earth has been given to me.

Therefore go and make disciples of all nations.

Baptizing them in the name of the Father and of the Son and of the Holy Spirit.

Teaching them to obey everything I have commanded you.

---

1. This idea comes from *The Life and Ministry of Jesus Christ, Book III* (Colorado Springs, CO: Navpress, 1977), p. 81.

And surely I will be with you always, to the very end of the age.

III. THE GREAT COMMISSION AND YOU

What challenge does the Great Commission give to you personally?

What can you do to begin to fulfill the Great Commission during this next week?

Who in your life needs your love, care, and witness of Jesus Christ? List three people.

When Christ ascended into heaven He entrusted the job of making disciples to people like yourself. What makes this Great Commission such an awesome task?

How do Jesus' words in Matthew 28:20 assure you of His help?

There is absolutely nothing greater or more challenging in life than to be used by God. Beginning the process of fulfilling the Great Commission with your life requires obedience and availability to God. *You can be used by God. GO FOR IT!*

12. The Ascension of Jesus

I. THE EVENT

    So when they met together, they asked him, "Lord, are you at this time going to restore the kingdom to Israel?"
    He said to them: "It is not for you to know the times or dates the Father has set by His own authority. But you will receive power when the Holy Spirit comes on you; and you will be my witnesses in Jerusalem, and in all Judea and Samaria, and to the ends of the earth."
    After he said this, he was taken up before their very eyes, and a cloud hid him from their sight.
    They were looking intently up into the sky as he was going, when suddenly two men dressed in white stood beside them. "Men of Galilee," they said, "why do you stand here looking into the sky? This same Jesus, who has been taken from you into heaven, will come back in the same way you have seen him go into heaven."

Acts 1:6-11

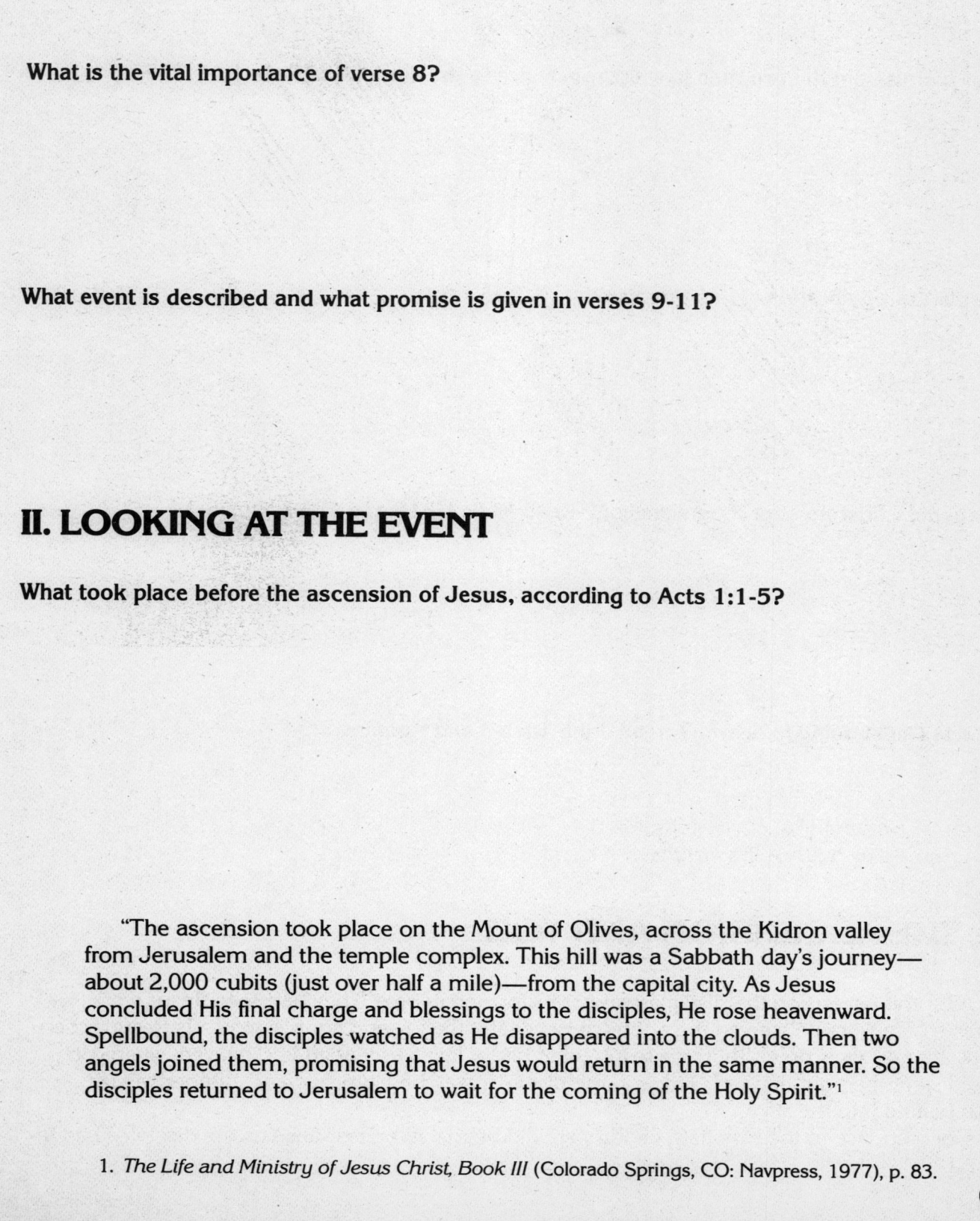

How did Jesus respond to the disciples' question in verse 6?

What is the vital importance of verse 8?

What event is described and what promise is given in verses 9-11?

II. LOOKING AT THE EVENT

What took place before the ascension of Jesus, according to Acts 1:1-5?

"The ascension took place on the Mount of Olives, across the Kidron valley from Jerusalem and the temple complex. This hill was a Sabbath day's journey—about 2,000 cubits (just over half a mile)—from the capital city. As Jesus concluded His final charge and blessings to the disciples, He rose heavenward. Spellbound, the disciples watched as He disappeared into the clouds. Then two angels joined them, promising that Jesus would return in the same manner. So the disciples returned to Jerusalem to wait for the coming of the Holy Spirit."[1]

1. *The Life and Ministry of Jesus Christ, Book III* (Colorado Springs, CO: Navpress, 1977), p. 83.

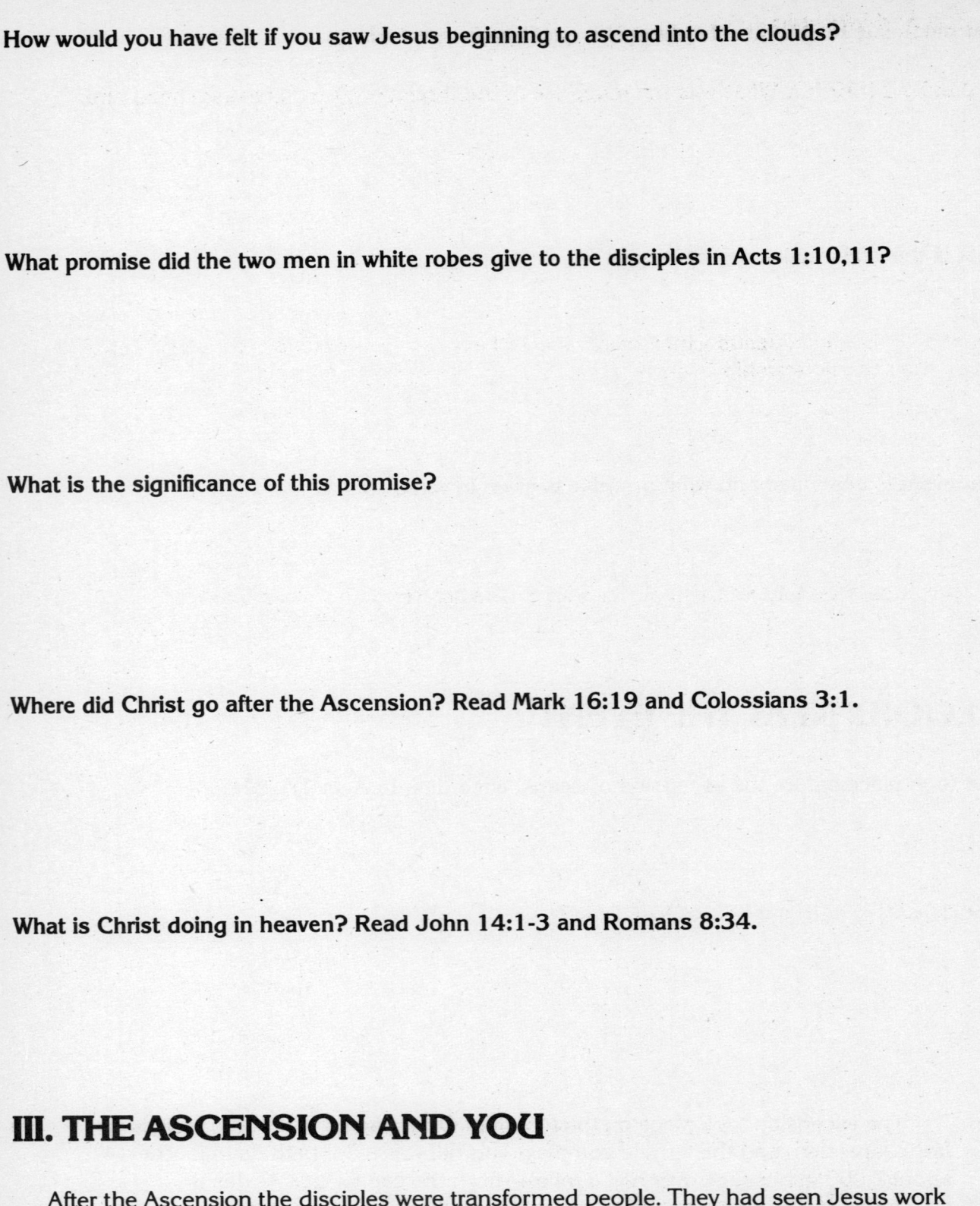

How would you have felt if you saw Jesus beginning to ascend into the clouds?

What promise did the two men in white robes give to the disciples in Acts 1:10,11?

What is the significance of this promise?

Where did Christ go after the Ascension? Read Mark 16:19 and Colossians 3:1.

What is Christ doing in heaven? Read John 14:1-3 and Romans 8:34.

III. THE ASCENSION AND YOU

After the Ascension the disciples were transformed people. They had seen Jesus work miracles. They had observed the agony of His death, the joy and confusion of His Resurrection. Now, after 40 days on earth in His resurrected body, Jesus ascended into heaven, where He would sit at the right hand of God, and the disciples watched, amazed and stunned, as He disappeared into the sky.

Our response in the twentieth century should be the same response as the disciples had in 33 A.D.:

(1) Joy and Worship

Read Luke 24:50-53. What was the response of the disciples after Jesus ascended into heaven?

How can this study of Jesus Christ cause you to have deeply rooted joy and a new sense of appreciation as you worship God?

What steps can you take to make joy and worship a greater part of your life?

(2) Power

What did Jesus tell His disciples in Acts 1:8 about power?

What kind of power is He talking about in this verse?

How would this power help your life?

What steps can you take to empower your life with the Holy Spirit?

(3) Proclamation

According to Mark 16:19,20, what did the disciples do when Jesus was taken up to heaven?

The word *proclamation* means to announce, tell, or preach. The disciples proclaimed everywhere the Resurrection, and the new life available in Jesus.

How do you think joy, worship, and power relate to proclaiming the good news of Christ?

Who do you know who needs to have proclaimed to them the good news of Jesus Christ?

Remember, proclamation is not only preaching from a pulpit at church. Often the best proclamation of the good news of Christ happens in daily living—over lunch, on a walk, perhaps while shopping.

This week focus on the wonderful events of Jesus Christ, and leave room in your busy schedule for **joy, worship,** receiving God's **power,** and **proclaiming** the good news.